D1447402

Conflict

....

A Redemptive Opportunity

Timothy S. Lane

New
Growth
Press

newgrowthpress.com

New Growth Press, Greensboro, NC 27404
Copyright © 2006 by Timothy S. Lane.
All rights reserved.

Cover Design: The DesignWorks Group, Nate Salciccioli and
Jeff Miller, www.thedesignworksgroup.com

Typesetting: Robin Black, www.blackbirdcreative.biz

ISBN-10: 0-9785567-0-4
ISBN-13: 978-0-9785567-0-9

Printed in India

28 27 26 25 24 23 22 21   17 18 19 20 21

The hardest thing to do is stick together.
Mates, family, marriage, business, bands. . . .
It's like resisting gravity. The alternative is
too predictable. You rid the room of argument.
You empty your life of the people you need the most.
BONO, U2 LEAD SINGER

None of us live in a world where conflict does not exist. It is unavoidable. Since that is the case, it makes sense to face the fact that you *will* have conflict. Admitting this opens the door for conflict to become a redemptive opportunity to mature in Christ. Some basic perspectives can help us as we tackle the tough issues involved.

Five Preliminary Perspectives

1. *The Bible is a story with conflict as a central theme.*
Conflict is not necessarily bad. In fact, there is a way to do conflict that is pleasing to God. One theme that runs from Genesis to Revelation is the theme of conflict and war—and God is the Warrior! He battles against the darkness and chaos of sin and suffering. Ultimately, Jesus joins the fight and gets bloody and dies. But he emerges as Victor over the forces of darkness through his death and resurrection. He opens the way for

enemies like us to be forgiven and reconciled to him, and then invites us to join him in battle. Ephesians 6:10–20 calls Christians to take up arms against sin and darkness in the same way Jesus did: through humility, love, and self-sacrifice. We are promised that one day Jesus will return, not riding on a donkey as in his first coming, but riding a white stallion. He will come to finish his redemptive work of conflict once for all.

2. *Conflict is an opportunity.* James 1:2–4 says that trials are an opportunity to grow. Most of us think of conflict as something to avoid, but conflict is a trial that gives us an opportunity to grow in tremendous ways. In fact, James says that without such trials, we will remain immature, incomplete, and lacking many godly character qualities. While conflict will rarely be fun, it should be seen as an opportunity to grow in grace.

3. *The person with whom you are in conflict is there for a divine purpose.* When a conflict is severe, this idea can be hard to swallow. But the truth remains: God, who is sovereign, loving, and wise, sends people into our lives so that he might work in us in ways that can only happen in conflict.

Remembering this protects us from demonizing the person in conflict with us. Even if the person is truly evil and sinning in malicious ways, while we are to be wise, we do not have the option to demonize him, write him off, and view him as beyond the reach of God's redeeming grace. Only God can see these things.

4. *There will be times when you will reach an impasse in conflict.* Being realistic does not minimize your responsibility, but it does remind you that not all conflict will be resolved this side of Christ's return. In Acts 15:36–41, Paul and Barnabas disagreed over whether John Mark should accompany them on Paul's second missionary journey. Barnabas and John Mark went their way together while Paul and Silas went in another direction. There will be times when you, too, will be limited in your ability to reconcile with others. We should not let this be an excuse to stop trying to resolve our differences. But it does remind us that we are limited in our ability to change others.

5. *You must get to the heart of conflict.* Without this emphasis, you minimize the conflict, settle for quick solutions that don't last, and avoid the hard work

of godly self-examination where God wants to see you grow. When you stay on the surface and avoid looking honestly at yourself, you bypass the centrality of the gospel and your need for Christ's grace.

Conflict and James 4

No passage in the Bible diagnoses the cause and cure of conflict like James 4. It looks at conflict's ugly underbelly but it also brims with optimism, showing us a redeeming God in relentless pursuit of his children. As you walk through this passage, you will see that it answers the questions that beg for answers in the midst of conflict. Its answers are not always the ones we *want* to hear, but they are exactly what we *need* to hear.

The Cause of Ungodly Conflict

Rob could be very impatient with his wife and children, especially at the end of a hard day. He would come home from work, longing to get away from the pressures of daily life. He was going through a tough transition at work and was more agitated than normal. Sleepless nights were also taking a toll.

One evening Rob was set on a calm evening without distractions. But as he came in the door, several of his children were arguing, the phone was ringing, and his wife was noticeably irritated that he was late. That's when it unraveled. Rob began to yell at his children, "I am sick and tired of this mess and noise when I come home from work. All I ask for is a little peace and quiet." Looking at his wife, Rob said, "I am out of here. I'll come back once I cool off and you get this place under control. Until then, I am not speaking to you!" In response, Rob's wife, Nina, grew cold and bitter as she reflected on the way she had been treated.

Here are two people engaged in conflict and doing it in very different but equally ungodly ways. Rob is aggressive in his anger. Nina is passive, fluctuating between withdrawing from Rob and trying everything she can think of to make him happy. She is growing tired of trying.

What is wrong here? Some might say that neither Rob nor Nina are getting their *legitimate* needs met. That is why they fight. The solution, in that case, would be to help them meet the other's needs to avoid this kind of warfare. Rob has a right to a clean and quiet house and Nina has a right to respect and civil treatment. What is tricky about this diagnosis and cure is that it skims the surface of truth but does not go deep enough. What would you say the problem is? How would you help Rob and Nina?

The Real Problem: Proper Diagnosis

James 4 begins by diagnosing the true problem, which will lead to a genuine cure. James does not waste any time as he bears down on the real problem in verses 1–3:

> What causes fights and quarrels among you? *Don't they come from your desires that battle within you?* You want something but don't get it. You kill and covet, but you cannot have what you want. You quarrel and fight. You do not have, because you do not ask God. When you ask, you do not receive, because you ask with wrong motives, that you may spend what you get on your pleasures. (emphasis added)

James asks the obvious question. Why do you fight? His answer is the opposite of what we often say. He says the problem is on the *inside* of each person! He does not talk about each person's circumstances, but rather what is going on in each person's heart: "Don't they come from your desires that battle within you?" There is war on the outside because there is war on the inside. Something has become so important to each person that each will do whatever it takes to get what he or she wants.

How many times have you said, "I would be more patient *if you* would do what I say"? James says the real problem is that a *desire*[1] for something has grown from a simple desire into a self-centered, sinful demand. A simple *desire* for a quiet home has morphed into a sinful *demand* for a quiet home. When Rob does not get what he wants, he lashes out. Nina's simple desire for a gentle husband has morphed into a sinful *demand* for one.[2] Ironically, neither is getting what he or she wants. Instead, both are intensifying the problem. This is how sin blinds and enslaves us as we get entangled in the web we have woven!

Below are a few typical desires that become all-consuming demands:

- **Comfort.** I want, must have, and deserve some rest and relaxation and you'd better not hinder my ability to get it!
- **Approval.** I want, must have, and deserve your approval and you'd better give it to me!
- **Success.** I want, must have, and deserve to be successful and I'll do anything to achieve it.
- **Power.** I want, must have and deserve power, and I will do anything to have it.

Most of us do not articulate our selfish desires quite like this, but our behavior speaks volumes.

Three Ungodly Strategies[3]

Different people use different strategies to get what they want. The same person can also use different strategies at different times. Here are three typical types of behavior that can be employed to satisfy one's selfish desires:

- **Win.** This strategy is typically chosen by people who like power, success, or comfort. This person hates failure, discomfort, and being out of control.
- **Please.** This strategy is typically favored by people who need approval. They tend to be quick to agree and have a hard time saying no because they fear rejection. They are often overcommitted.
- **Avoid.** This strategy is typically used by people who want approval or comfort. Living alone has benefits for this person—no possibility of rejection and no discomfort!

Do you see yourself in these strategies? Most of us see a little of ourselves in all of them, to varying degrees. One strategy may be more pronounced in you than the others. If you recognize yourself, you are ready to see the cure James provides!

The Cure: Growing towards Godly Conflict

Step 1: Self-Examination (James 4:1–3)
Before you can begin the cure, you must diagnose

the disease. The difference between ungodly and godly conflict starts with the ability to see the log in your own eye. This includes both heart and behavior. Why is this so important? The answer is in verses 2 and 3. Verse 3 says that these ungodly ruling desires eclipse your love for God, so that either you don't pray or you pray with selfish motives. Verse 2 says that you fail to love your neighbor. When ungodly desires rule, you break the first and second great commandments. This serious sin lies at the heart of your conflict.

Big Question #1: What do I want right now more than Christ and how am I acting to get it?

Step 2: Engage in Intelligent Repentance and Faith (James 4:4–6, 8)

Once you have done the hard work of self-examination (a work of grace in itself), you are ready for the redemptive promises in verses 4–6. These verses enable us to "purify our hearts" (v. 8) since that is where the real problem lies. They brim with hope.

> You adulterous people, don't you know that friendship with the world is hatred toward God? Anyone who chooses to be a friend of the world becomes an enemy of God. Or do you think Scripture says without reason that the spirit

he caused to live in us envies intensely? But he gives us more grace. That is why Scripture says: "God opposes the proud but gives grace to the humble."

Verse 4 restates what verses 1–3 outlined. Because you have made something more important than God, you are in an extramarital relationship, spiritually speaking. You have become an unfaithful bride to your true husband, Jesus. While this is a negative assessment, notice how this verse talks about your relationship with God. If you belong to Jesus, you are in a marriage relationship with him! In one sense, this verse is a reminder of who your true love and husband is. It is also a reminder of who *you* are—the beloved of God. This is not because of anything you have done, but because of his mercy and grace. These verses call you to remember your true identity. In addition, verse 5 says that when you stray, God is a jealous lover who will not let you share your love and affection with another. He sends his Spirit to reclaim your heart's devotion and then gives you even more grace when you humble yourself (v. 6)![4]

James is saying that even God's children can stray from their love and devotion to God. Yet when you do, he loves you so much that he will not sit by and tolerate it. He does not drop the hammer and judge you; instead, he pursues you with a holy love so that you will be captivated by his love for you at the very moment you are being unfaithful.

What does this have to do with "intelligent repentance and faith"? When you are most conscious of God's love for you in Christ, you are most willing to look at the false love that has replaced your love for him. You are ready to ask specific questions about why you are in conflict with another person. You can begin to ask some specific questions about your motivation and behavior. Looking inward moves you outward to see Christ and his grace. The more dazzling his grace becomes, the less attractive your god replacements seem. You begin repenting of what has dislodged God from his rightful place in your life. You also believe and grasp how great Christ's grace is. This is the dynamic that leads to lasting change. James 4:7–10 outlines what it looks like to repent of sin (heart and hands/motivation and behavior) and believe in Christ:

> Submit yourselves, then, to God. Resist the
> devil, and he will flee from you. Come near to
> God and he will come near to you. Wash your
> hands, you sinners, and purify your hearts,
> you double-minded. Grieve, mourn and wail.
> Change your laughter to mourning and your
> joy to gloom. Humble yourselves before the
> Lord, and he will lift you up.

In verse 4, James called you to repent of making something in this *world* more important to you than God. In verses 7–10, he calls you to resist the *devil* and *remaining sin* in your heart. It is a battle cry to wage war by the Spirit against the world, the flesh, and the devil. As you do, you will be lifted up. God loves humble people and he loves to shower his grace on the humble of heart.

Big Question #2: What specifically do I need to repent of? What do I need to ask for in terms of grace? What has hijacked my heart, and what do I need to see and believe about Christ?

Step 3: Consider the Other Person

Though James does not mention this explicitly, we know that honest self-examination and repentance enable you to see your neighbor better, too! If ungodly ruling desires blind you to your neighbor (v. 2), a pure heart will bring that same neighbor back to your mind's eye. Whenever God enables us to reorient ourselves vertically toward him, according to the first great commandment (love your God with all your heart), we are then more likely to obey the second great commandment (love your neighbor) as well.

For example, in 1 Peter 3:7–8 Peter is encouraging husbands to love their wives. The application is specific to husbands, but he then applies the principle to all believers. Notice what Peter says:

> Husbands, in the same way be considerate as you live with your wives, and treat them with respect as the weaker partner and as heirs with you of the gracious gift of life, so that nothing will hinder your prayers. Finally, all of you, live in harmony with one another; be sympathetic, love as brothers, be compassionate and humble.

Peter calls husbands to live with their wives with *consideration.* The best way to translate this powerful word is to use the metaphor of living in the other person's shoes or skin. Peter is urging husbands to live with their wives in such a way that they know what it must feel like for their wives to be married to them![5] In light of this passage, it is clear that a key ingredient to godly conflict is to understand the other person.

Big Question #3: What is your experience as you enter into conflict with me right now? Is it a good experience or a bad one?

Step 4: Move toward the Person in Love
Deep and thorough repentance and faith take you out of the center of things and enable you to see those

around you. You now see them through eyes cleansed by the forgiving grace of Christ. You begin to see things that, in your sin, you were not able to see. You may not ignore sin if it is there, but you begin to see the person and the struggles, temptations, and weaknesses that are part of his conflict with you. At this point, you can choose to serve and not be served. Christ's massive service for you on the cross gets bigger; it progressively changes your heart and empowers you to serve the other person. Many passages guide us in this direction, such as 1 Corinthians 13, Galatians 5:22–26, and Colossians 3:12–17. Any of these may help you think about what love in action will look like. A passage that richly nuances the ways love can be expressed amid conflict is 1 Thessalonians 5:14–18:

> And we urge you, brothers, warn those who are idle, encourage the timid, help the weak, be patient with everyone. Make sure that nobody pays back wrong for wrong, but always try to be kind to each other and to everyone else. Be joyful always; pray continually; give thanks in all circumstances, for this is God's will for you in Christ Jesus.

Paul is giving pastoral instruction to the Thessalonians as they seek to help each other grow in grace. These short verses provide practical guidance as you seek to serve someone who is in conflict with you.

Warn the idle. Love warns someone when there are patterns of destructive behavior that involve obvious violations of God's wise and loving commands. In 1 Thessalonians, these Christians were likely avoiding work because they thought the Lord's coming was imminent. Paul warns these brothers and sisters in 4:11–12.[6]

If we were to apply this principle to Rob, we would begin with the fact that his anger is not a small matter, but a serious breach of the sixth commandment: "Do not murder." His anger is a form of murder and a lack of love with serious ramifications for his family. If Nina really loves Rob, she will make every attempt to help him see the seriousness of his anger. If she is afraid of him, she will need other godly people to love Rob by inviting him to seek Christ's grace for his sin. Whenever there is a persistent pattern of sin, love requires us to move toward the person with gentle courage and humble resolve.

Nina may need to be warned as well. If she has become hardened and bitter towards Rob, she too is guilty of breaking the sixth commandment. Though Rob is the perpetrator and Nina is often sinned against, she faces many temptations to seek revenge.

Encourage the timid. Love comes alongside the fearful and brings encouragement. More than likely, Paul has in mind those who were weak in their faith. They were worried about the salvation of their deceased loved ones and possibly their own salvation too.[7] If you look at the entire letter of 1 Thessalonians, it is a letter of encouragement to those struggling to live the Christian life amid significant difficulty. Paul encourages them in 4:13—5:10.

Rob and Nina need to be reminded of the powerful grace of Christ that is theirs. They need to be reminded that Jesus is a King who will not stop working in them until everything opposed to him is overthrown and dismantled. He will settle for nothing short of complete maturity. He is committed to making them into what he is. This is the hope Rob and Nina need as they work through their conflict.

Help the weak. Love sometimes calls us to hold someone's hand as she grows in her faith. More than likely, Paul is referring to believers who were finding sexual control difficult (1 Thessalonians 4:3–8). These Christians need help.[8] The word *help* can be translated: "Hold on to them," "Cling to them," or "Put your arm round them."[9] This figurative way of speaking emphasizes their need for practical guidance and support through the long process of change. Notice that Paul's help has backbone to it, but he remains sensitive to the fact that these are brothers and sisters who have come out of a reckless lifestyle. They need to be reminded of the gospel's comfort as well as its call.

Nina needs others to come alongside her as she seeks to love Rob. Rob has also sought help and accountability. He wants to change, but he tends to give up when he blows it. Help holds someone's hand and shows him what to do. Good teaching and modeling are necessary to help the weak person: "Let me tell you *and* show you what it will look like for you to change."

Be patient. Real love is persistent. We are called to be longsuffering with the idle, timid, and weak. That means we are to warn, encourage, and help one another for a really, really long time! Change does not happen in us or others overnight. Most of the time, it is a slow, progressive process with many ups and downs. With whom are you in conflict? Have you ever been tempted to say, "I have done all these things and nothing has changed"? Then keep on doing those things. If the person has not changed due to hard-heartedness and clear rejection of the truth, it will be appropriate for the church to assist you and the other person in light of Matthew 18:15–20. But even this is to be done with great care and love.

Revoke revenge. Love revokes revenge and practices forgiveness.[10] A great temptation in conflict is to gradually give up hope and grow self-righteous and angry at the other person. We are called to reject this temptation and do good to those in conflict with us.

Worship. How is all this possible? Paul brings us full circle in 1 Thessalonians 5:16–17 by calling us to worship! "Be joyful always; pray continually; give thanks in all circumstances, for this is God's will for you in Christ Jesus." This is a call to first commandment reorientation. Because we are always tempted by ungodly ruling desires, our worship of God must be regular. This includes formal worship as well as worship as a lifestyle, encompassing all of life every moment, every day! To engage in godly conflict, I must be captivated by the grace of Christ. This will lead to joy, spontaneous and persistent prayer, and an ability to give thanks in all circumstances—even the circumstance of conflict!

Big Question #4: "What will it look like to wisely love the person in conflict with me? Will I warn, encourage, or help?"

Step 5: Make a Plan
If you don't have a concrete plan that grows out of what we have been describing, you may miss the greatest

part of godly conflict: to come through it with a new way of relating to one another that sets a course for new trust and stability in the relationship. Here are some specific, concrete actions:

- **Understand the problem.** It is important for both parties to name the problem. This by itself may bring greater clarity and help. There may be more than one problem, so it is important to deal with one problem at a time.
- **Self-examination.** Work through the "Big Questions." If the relationship can handle it, you may want to do this together.
- **Seek and grant forgiveness.** Own your sin and ask for forgiveness. If the other person asks for forgiveness, be willing to grant it.
- **Explore possible solutions.** Discuss possible alternatives and solutions to the problem. Name some and choose one.
- **Implement a solution.** Discuss how you plan to implement the solution. When will you begin? What responsibilities will each person have? Set a time to meet again to evaluate how the solution worked or did not work.
- **Evaluate.** Assess how your plan worked. If it didn't, ask why. If it did, make a commitment to continue to grow.

- **Agree to get outside help if needed.** If you make several attempts to resolve the conflict, be open and willing to seek outside help. This should be a mature Christian trusted by both parties.

Conflict is rarely fun, but godly conflict can be redemptive in us and in those in conflict with us. Cast yourself on Christ's mercy and grace. Ask him to make you a more humble and wise Christian as you love others in the midst of conflict. By all means, do everything you can to keep from "emptying your life of the people you need the most"!

Endnotes

1. The word James uses here is *hedone*. We get our word *hedonism* from this word. It does not always connote something bad but, in many contexts, it implies sinful envy. Our strong desires get allied with our sinful nature, and they morph into something that replaces the centrality of the living God in our lives. Most books on marital conflict say that the number one problem in marriage is poor communication, or pressures brought on by finances, children, or sex. But these are symptoms of a deeper problem. They can certainly contribute to the downward spiral of the relationship and immediate intervention is appropriate, but the diagnosis cannot stop there. That is what James has in mind. For further discussion see Alec Motyer's *The Message of James: The Bible Speaks Today* (Downers Grove, IL: InterVarsity Press, 1985), p. 142.

2. Please note that we are not minimizing what Rob is doing to Nina. At this point, we are simply diagnosing the problem. There are significant pastoral issues that need to be addressed and church involvement by wise leadership may very well be needed. This would be part of the cure. If you don't diagnose this relationship rightly, you could wrongly conclude that Nina needs to be more organized and compliant while Rob needs to simmer down, which would downplay the serious spiritual malady present in this marriage.

3. I am indebted to John Bettler and Winston Smith for these insights.

4. These are not easy verses to translate, but I think I have faithfully captured the emphasis taught here.

5. Some have interpreted this verse to mean that women are weaker emotionally and physically, but the context does not seem to make that argument. Rather, it seems to emphasize that women were more vulnerable in this culture because they were in the place of submission. Husbands were to be very careful about how they treated their wives since husbands were in a position of greater power. Notice, too, that Peter emphasizes that wives are equal in terms of being heirs of grace.

6. John Stott, *The Message of I and II Thessalonians* (Downers Grove, IL: InterVarsity Press, 1991), p. 122. These believers were freeloading on the community and bringing shame to the church and the name of Christ.

7. Ibid., p. 122.

8. Ibid., p. 122.

9. Ibid., p. 122.

10. A more detailed description of forgiveness can be found in another booklet in this series entitled, *Forgiving Others: Joining Wisdom and Love.*